100

PRAYERS
F O R   Y O U R
MARRIAGE

Draw Close to Each Other
and Closer to God

New York Times Best-Selling Author
Darlene Schacht

The Ministry of Time-Warp Wife
www.timewarpwife.com

All Scripture unless otherwise noted is taken from The KJV
Bible

100 Prayers for Your Marriage: Draw Close to Each Other
and Closer to God

Time-Warp Wife
Suite 5-1377 Border Street
Winnipeg, Manitoba
R3H 0N1

Copyright © 2015 by Darlene Schacht

ISBN: 978-0-9780262-4-0

Cover design by Darlene Schacht
Image from Bigstock.com

Find Darlene Schacht on the web here:
Blog: TimeWarpWife.com
Facebook: timewarpwife
Twitter: timewarpwife
Pinterest: timewarpwife

If you enjoy this book, please leave a review at Amazon.

Contents

Introduction

When I was a teenager, both my sister and I started a "hope chest." Every so often we'd fill it with hand-me-downs in hopes that one day we'd carry these treasures into homes we'd each call our own. I think I had a few pots, some old china, a stack of recipe cards, and a blanket in there.

Eventually I did get married. The contents of the box were carefully unpacked along with the new towels, cutlery, and bedding we purchased. But there was something missing in that box, in fact I didn't unpack this treasure until years later when I realized that prayer is the most valuable gem that a marriage could ever possess.

Sure I bowed my head and said thanks for my food. I even thanked God for my husband and home. But I was missing out on the power of fervent prayer.

James 5:16 tells us, "the effectual fervent prayer of a righteous man availeth much."

Do you see that word "fervent" there? That means that we're going to be enthusiastic about prayer. That tells me that prayer is something we're looking forward to. That says, I'm excited about praying for my marriage and I'm not going to give up on this man (or for you guys who are reading this – "I'm not giving up on this woman").

Sometimes I ask my kids to check if the water is boiling on the stove. They'll often say, "I'm not sure. I see some bubbles coming up."

Here's my answer to them, "When it's boiling, you'll know it's boiling. There's no mistaking it."

Let's be that fervent when it comes to our prayer life.

Let there be no mistaking the fact that you've brought your marriage before God and placed it at the foot of His throne.

Get down on your knees if you want to or stand up with your hands raised to God. Whatever you say, and however you pray, do it with all of your might. Pour yourself out to God and let His Spirit pour back into you.

Prayer is effective. And if you are walking in a right relationship with God, it's all the more effective.Be cautious of this as Psalm 66:18 warns, "If I regard iniquity in my heart, the Lord will not hear my prayer."

Don't let the enemy get his foot in the door, and if he does have a foot in the door? The Bible tells us to "Submit yourselves therefore to God. Resist the devil, and he will flee from you." (James 4:7). Start eliminating each and every one of those negative thoughts as you turn your focus to God.

Bring your husband before God praying for each and every burden you carry, then trust that He will do a work in your marriage.

Pray for a hedge of protection around your marriage and keep praying for that day after day.

Psalm 91:9-11 tells us, "If you make the Lord your refuge, if you make the Most High your shelter, no evil will conquer you; no plague will come near your home. For he shall give his angels charge over thee, to keep thee in all thy ways."

If you're marriage is good--praise God, but also remember this truth,

"Be sober, be vigilant; because your adversary the devil, as a roaring lion, walketh about, seeking whom he may devour:" – 1 Peter 5:8

We're told in Job 1:10 that Job had a hedge of protection, but Satan desired to test him. Your marriage could be tested at any time, which is why fervent prayer is the most important thing you can unpack in your marriage.

- O N E -

Our Outside Relationships

Dear Heavenly Father,

Please help us to build healthy friendships. Bring people into our lives that will encourage us and strengthen us in our faith. And may we also encourage our friends in their faith.

May we be trustworthy friends who love others well.

Help us to connect with new friends and to open our home to those who need fellowship.

Open our eyes to the unexpected, so that we might see people in the light of Your will.

When we are with friends, may we have fun, but may our conversation also bring glory and honor to You.

And finally, Lord, thank you for being our unfailing friend and trustworthy companion.

In the name of Jesus we pray. Amen.

And it came to pass, when he had made an end of speaking unto Saul, that the soul of Jonathan was knit with the soul of David, and Jonathan loved him as his own soul. And Saul took him that day, and would let him go no more home to his father's house.

Then Jonathan and David made a covenant, because he loved him as his own soul. And Jonathan stripped himself of the robe that was upon him, and gave it to David, and his garments, even to his sword, and to his bow, and to his girdle.

1 Samuel 18:1-4

- TWO -
To Heal

Dear Heavenly Father,

Please teach us how to forgive. Your word tells us to forgive others as You have also forgiven us.

We need to let go of our anger, our hurt, and our pain so that we can move forward, Lord. Please help us to do that.

Help us to let go of resentment, and soften our hearts to choose love. Give us the wisdom to handle our pain wisely and to draw boundaries where they need to be drawn.

If we are angry, may we harness that anger so we don't sin against You. And when we are hurt, please help us to heal.

In the name of Jesus we pray. Amen.

Be ye angry, and sin not: let not the sun go down upon your wrath: neither give place to the devil.

Ephesians 4:26-27

- THREE -
To Hold Fast to Our Vows

Dear Heavenly Father,

Grant us the strength to hold fast to our vows. When we got married we promised to love, honor, and cherish each other as long as we both shall live. And so we ask that you teach us to love the way that we should, with patience and kindness, forgiveness and grace.

Show us the best way to bestow honor one to another.

Open our hearts to fully cherish each other, and open our eyes to see the blessings we have.

Finally, Lord, may we never take these vows for granted, but rather fulfill them with honor and strength.

In the name of Jesus we pray. Amen.

And whosoever doth not bear his cross, and come after me, cannot be my disciple.

For which of you, intending to build a tower, sitteth not down first, and counteth the cost, whether he have sufficient to finish it?

Luke 14:27-28

- FOUR -
To Trust God With Tomorrow

Dear Heavenly Father,

Thank you for Your unfailing grace. Please help us to let go of those things that we need to leave in the past, and to start moving forward in faith.

May we always see Your hand at work in our future and trust You with every tomorrow. We don't know what the future will bring, but we do know that You'll be there beside us whatever may come.

Please remove the burden of any pain that we carry. Replace it with hope. Give us the wisdom we need to see the light on our path, and grant us the courage to follow Your voice.

In the name of Jesus we pray. Amen.

I am the Lord, your Holy One, the creator of Israel, your King. Thus saith the Lord, which maketh a way in the sea, and a path in the mighty waters; which bringeth forth the chariot and horse, the army and the power; they shall lie down together, they shall not rise: they are extinct, they are quenched as tow.

Isaiah 43:15-17

FIVE

For Pure Thoughts

Dear Heavenly Father,

Give us pure thoughts, and guide us to reflect on them carefully.

Your word tells us not to be conformed to this world, but to be transformed by the renewing of our minds. And so we ask that You help us to do this Lord. Give us a hunger and thirst for righteousness, so that we might meditate on Your word. For we know that righteous living must start from within before it moves out.

Protect us from the temptation to entertain thoughts that we shouldn't, and give us the wisdom to feed our minds well.

In the name of Jesus we pray. Amen.

Finally, brethren, whatsoever things are true, whatsoever things are honest, whatsoever things are just, whatsoever things are pure, whatsoever things are lovely, whatsoever things are of good report; if there be any virtue, and if there be any praise, think on these things. Those things, which ye have both learned, and received, and heard, and seen in me, do: and the God of peace shall be with you.

Philippians 4:8-9

- SIX -
For Joy

Dear Heavenly Father,

Please bless our marriage with an abundance of joy. We started off strong, and it's our deepest desire that we finish that way.

Some couples go through life barely communicating, hardly enjoying each other's company, and missing out on the many blessings that marriage can bring.

We want more for our marriage. We want to be able to laugh together and to enjoy this journey we're on. Remind us to look for joy and to choose it over our sorrow. As long as we're living, may we always find a reason to smile.

Keep our friendship alive, keep the romance alive, and keep this spark between us alive.

In the name of Jesus we pray. Amen.

O Lord, thou hast brought up my soul from the grave: thou hast kept me alive, that I should not go down to the pit.

Sing unto the Lord, O ye saints of his, and give thanks at the remembrance of his holiness.

For his anger endureth but a moment; in his favour is life: weeping may endure for a night, but joy cometh in the morning.

Psalm 30:3-4

SEVEN

On Behalf of Others

Dear Heavenly Father,

We come before you today on behalf of marriages that are broken and those that are wounded and hurt.

A marriage is never beyond repair. There is always hope for those who put their trust in You, and so we stand in the gap for these couples, Lord, asking that you would restore the love between them. Tear down walls where they've been built, and heal each broken heart.

We ask that You would grant understanding and wisdom to those who are going through tough times. Teach them how to forgive, and how to rebuild what they've lost.

In the name of Jesus we pray. Amen.

For this reason I bow my knees to the Father of our Lord Jesus Christ, from whom the whole family in heaven and earth is named, that He would grant you, according to the riches of His glory, to be strengthened with might through His Spirit in the inner man, that Christ may dwell in your hearts through faith; that you, being rooted and grounded in love, may be able to comprehend with all the saints what is the width and length and depth and height—to know the love of Christ which passes knowledge; that you may be filled with all the fullness of God.

Now to Him who is able to do exceedingly abundantly above all that we ask or think, according to the power that works in us, to Him be glory in the church by Christ Jesus to all generations, forever and ever. Amen.

Ephesians 3:14-21

- EIGHT -
Our Differences

Dear Heavenly Father,

Help us to accept our differences. Help us to see the unique way that You formed us, and to understand that we were both created according to plan.

Please help us to nurture the gifts we see in each other. And may those gifts be sharpened and strengthened and used for Your glory.

Neither of us are perfect, which is why we need your strength in our lives. Our personalities are different, and sometimes those differences bring hurt and confusion. So we ask that you teach us to love as You love, with patience and grace.

Grant us the humility to see what we need to improve, and wisdom to make those changes.

In the name of Jesus we pray. Amen.

We then that are strong ought to bear the infirmities of the weak, and not to please ourselves. Let every one of us please his neighbour for his good to edification. For even Christ pleased not himself; but, as it is written, The reproaches of them that reproached thee fell on me. For whatsoever things were written aforetime were written for our learning, that we through patience and comfort of the scriptures might have hope. Now the God of patience and consolation grant you to be likeminded one toward another according to Christ Jesus: That ye may with one mind and one mouth glorify God, even the Father of our Lord Jesus Christ. Wherefore receive ye one another, as Christ also received us to the glory of God.

Romans 15:1-7

- NINE -
Our Marriage Bed

Dear Heavenly Father,

As we seek to serve you in every area of our marriage, may we be affectionate in ways that are pleasing to You.

Ignite the passion between us. Give us the strength to keep our marriage pure, and teach us to love the way that we need to be loved.

May we never forget that our bodies belong to each other, and also to You.

Please remind us to cherish the physical part of our relationship so that we aren't leaving this important part of our marriage behind.

If we're tired, worn out, or stressed, remind us to be compassionate and understanding so that we can move through these seasons together.

In the name of Jesus we pray. Amen.

Let the husband render unto the wife due benevolence: and likewise also the wife unto the husband. The wife hath not power of her own body, but the husband: and likewise also the husband hath not power of his own body, but the wife. Defraud ye not one the other, except it be with consent for a time, that ye may give yourselves to fasting and prayer; and come together again, that Satan tempt you not for your incontinency.

1 Corinthians 7:3-5

TEN

For Disagreements

Dear Heavenly Father,

Please help us to resolve disagreements in ways that are pleasing to you. Give us the strength to lay down our anger and pride. Teach us to be gentle, and to handle each other with care.

If there is any fighting at all, may we be fighting together for all that is holy and just.

May we seek to please You more than we seek to please ourselves, or to be right, or to win an argument for the sake of our pride.

And may we always choose "we" over "me."

In the name of Jesus we pray. Amen.

I therefore, the prisoner of the Lord, beseech you that ye walk worthy of the vocation wherewith ye are called, with all lowliness and meekness, with longsuffering, forbearing one another in love; endeavouring to keep the unity of the Spirit in the bond of peace.

Ephesians 4:1-3

ELEVEN

To Glorify God

Dear Heavenly Father,

We pray that our marriage would glorify You, and that our covenant would be a reflection of the covenant You freely offer those who believe on Your son, Jesus Christ.

You word says that husbands are to love their wives as Christ loved the church and gave Himself up for it, and that a wife should submit to her husband as unto the Lord. Loving is easy until it requires us to lay down our lives and pick up our cross, and so we pray that You would give us strength as we seek to submit to Your will.

Let our marriage be a testimony. Not just one that merely testifies of our love, but one that points others to Yours.

In the name of Jesus we pray. Amen.

Then said Jesus unto his disciples, If any man will come after me, let him deny himself, and take up his cross, and follow me.

For whosoever will save his life shall lose it: and whosoever will lose his life for my sake shall find it.

For what is a man profited, if he shall gain the whole world, and lose his own soul? or what shall a man give in exchange for his soul?

Matthew 16:24-26

- TWELVE -
For Provision

Dear Heavenly Father,

Thank you for our home and everything in it. May we give thanks often, and trust that You'll provide for us, each day as it comes.

Give us a sense of peace when our finances are tight, and the wisdom to work our way through it.

Remind us to treasure the things that we have, knowing that all goodness stems from Your grace.

And when we don't have the things that we desperately want, teach us to patiently wait on Your will and Your timing. As the apostle Paul said, "I have learned, in whatsoever state I am, therewith to be content."

In the name of Jesus we pray. Amen.

Therefore take no thought, saying, What shall we eat?
or, What shall we drink? or, Wherewithal shall we be
clothed? (For after all these things do the Gentiles seek)
for your heavenly Father knoweth that ye have need of
all these things. But seek ye first the kingdom of God,
and his righteousness; and all these things shall be added
unto you. Take therefore no thought for the morrow: for
the morrow shall take thought for the things of itself.
Sufficient unto the day is the evil thereof.

Matthew 6:31-34

- THIRTEEN -
Teach Us to Pray

Dear Heavenly Father,

Teach us to pray, Lord.

We don't always know the right things to say, but we know that You do. You know what's best for our marriage, and so we ask that you would give us the words.

Remind us to pray throughout the day. There are so many moments—so many ups and downs in our lives—and so we want to remember to stop and give thanks to You, and to stop and ask for Your help.

May we be in a constant state of prayer, knowing You are always near and moving in our lives.

In the name of Jesus we pray. Amen.

After this manner therefore pray ye: Our Father which art in heaven, Hallowed be thy name. Thy kingdom come, Thy will be done in earth, as it is in heaven.

Give us this day our daily bread. And forgive us our debts, as we forgive our debtors.

And lead us not into temptation, but deliver us from evil: For thine is the kingdom, and the power, and the glory, for ever. Amen.

Matthew 6:9-13

- FOURTEEN -
For Kindness

Dear Heavenly Father,

Your Word says that love is patient and kind, and yet there are days when we're anything but patient, and hardly as kind as we should be.

We ask Your forgiveness, Lord. Please help us to grow.

Teach us to be united, to lean on You, and to stand strong when our lives are tested. May You remind us to be gentle and kind when things aren't going our way. Grant us the strength to keep our emotions in check and to cherish our marriage enough to walk in Your will.

In the name of Jesus I pray. Amen.

But the fruit of the Spirit is love, joy, peace, longsuffering, gentleness, goodness, faith,

Meekness, temperance: against such there is no law.

Galatians 5:22-23

- FIFTEEN -
Our In-Laws

Dear Heavenly Father,

Please help us to embrace each other's family as we would our own. Remind us to be kind and compassionate when people and situations are difficult.

As children honor their parents, may we also love and honor our in-laws. Give us the strength to accept the differences that we have, and the wisdom to keep peace in the family.

We want to respect them, Lord, but we also want to draw healthy boundaries, and so we ask for your guidance. Give us patience and wisdom as we seek to honor them in the best way we know how.

In the name of Jesus we pray. Amen.

And Adam said, This is now bone of my bones, and flesh of my flesh: she shall be called Woman, because she was taken out of Man.

Therefore shall a man leave his father and his mother, and shall cleave unto his wife: and they shall be one flesh.

Genesis 2: 23-24

- SIXTEEN -
Modern Technology

Dear Heavenly Father,

Please help us to set healthy boundaries with modern technology. Lord, You know that we live in a world where people are attached to their phones and glued to their screens. While these electronics are helpful, we know that they can also be harmful if they're not handled with wisdom and care.

Please teach us to draw lines where and when we should. Give us the wisdom to make good choices and the strength to use technology in moderation.

Guard our hearts from temptation. Keep us safe when we're searching. And if we do see something that we shouldn't Lord, may we have the strength and the wisdom to turn our eyes from sin, detesting that which is evil.

In the name of Jesus we pray. Amen.

P.S. If you have children, also pray that God would guard their hearts from temptation and keep them safe when they're searching. Ask Him to give you wisdom as parents in guiding your children through this technical age.

For the grace of God that bringeth salvation hath appeared to all men, teaching us that, denying ungodliness and worldly lusts, we should live soberly, righteously, and godly, in this present world; looking for that blessed hope, and the glorious appearing of the great God and our Saviour Jesus Christ; who gave himself for us, that he might redeem us from all iniquity, and purify unto himself a peculiar people, zealous of good works.

Titus 2:11-14

- S E V E N T E E N -
To See the Small Things

Dear Heavenly Father,

Please help us to show our appreciation for each other whether it's in the little things that we do or in grand gestures of love. Teach us to serve with gratitude and to give with a graceful heart.

Help us to see the small things and to offer thanks when we do. Help us to see the way that You do.

Give us eyes to see each other in beautiful ways that we've never noticed before.

Show us the unique qualities that only we have, and help us to appreciate each one of them.

In the name of Jesus we pray. Amen.

Be kindly affectioned one to another with brotherly love; in honour preferring one another; Not slothful in business; fervent in spirit; serving the Lord; Rejoicing in hope; patient in tribulation; continuing instant in prayer; Let love be without dissimulation. Abhor that which is evil; cleave to that which is good.

Romans 12:10-12

EIGHTEEN

For Gratitude

Dear Heavenly Father,

Thank You for Your many blessings. Please teach us to look for them each and every day. Remind us to give thanks, and to trust You completely when we're walking in darkness. We can't always see Your plan Lord, and we're learning that we don't always have to. Use us according to Your will.

We're grateful for Your unfailing grace and faithfulness. If we're led through trials, please teach us to lean on You, and to always give thanks.

In the name of Jesus we pray. Amen.

Enter into his gates with thanksgiving, and into his courts with praise: be thankful unto him, and bless his name.

For the Lord is good; his mercy is everlasting; and his truth endureth to all generations.

Psalm 100:4-5

- NINETEEN -
A Gentle Spirit

Dear Heavenly Father,

Please give us a gentle spirit, and remind us to handle each other with care. Whether we're having a good day, or the weight of the world is bringing us down, may we be tender and loving one to another.

May our words be gentle, our actions be kind, and our thoughts always tender and pure.

Let us be quick to hear, slow to speak, and slow to anger, looking to You as our perfect example. For You, oh Lord, are holy and just, gentle and kind.

In the name of Jesus we pray. Amen.

For where envying and strife is, there is confusion and every evil work. But the wisdom that is from above is first pure, then peaceable, gentle, and easy to be intreated, full of mercy and good fruits, without partiality, and without hypocrisy. And the fruit of righteousness is sown in peace of them that make peace.

James 3:16-18

TWENTY

Against Secular Views

Dear Heavenly Father,

We come before you today asking You to protect our hearts. Don't let us be swayed by secular views or give in to popular opinions of what marriage should look like.

Your Word is true and just and wise. Your blueprint for marriage is every bit as perfect as it was on the day You designed it.

We heed to the scripture that tells us no man should separate what You have brought together.

As difficult as it might be some days, we stand by Your Word, and we faithfully stand by our vows.

In the name of Jesus we pray. Amen.

But from the beginning of the creation God made them male and female. For this cause shall a man leave his father and mother, and cleave to his wife; and they twain shall be one flesh: so then they are no more twain, but one flesh. What therefore God hath joined together, let not man put asunder.

Mark 10:6-9

- TWENTY ONE -
To Encourage

Dear Heavenly Father,

Please teach us the best way to encourage each other. May one be strong when the other is weak, ready with a word of encouragement.

Help us to choose our words wisely and gently administer them.

We pray that our speech would have a positive affect on each other, and add strength to our marriage. We don't always know the best way to encourage or the right things to say, and so we ask for Your wisdom and strength.

Please shape us as we're growing each day. Equip us to be an encouraging couple, seasoned with grace and walking in truth.

In the name of Jesus we pray. Amen.

For God hath not appointed us to wrath, but to obtain salvation by our Lord Jesus Christ,

Who died for us, that, whether we wake or sleep, we should live together with him.

Wherefore comfort yourselves together, and edify one another, even as also ye do.

1 Thessalonians 5:9-11

TWENTY TWO

For Peace

Dear Heavenly Father,

We come before You today asking that You would fill us with a deep sense of peace.

Help us to find it on the darkest of days, and please give us the strength to choose it.

Teach us to trust when the future's unknown, and let each step we take be steady and sure.

Your word tells us not to be anxious about anything. It tells us to bring our burdens to You with thanksgiving and prayer.

But so many times we forget. Day after day we carry the weight of our sorrow until we're brought down to our knees in prayer.

Remind us to listen, Lord. Remind us to run to You first.

In the name of Jesus we pray. Amen.

Be careful for nothing; but in every thing by prayer and supplication with thanksgiving let your requests be made known unto God. And the peace of God, which passeth all understanding, shall keep your hearts and minds through Christ Jesus.

Philippians 4:6-7

TWENTY THREE

To Build

Dear Heavenly Father,

As clay in the hands of a potter, we surrender our lives. Lord, we ask that you mold us and make us into the couple You designed us to be.

Teach us how to build up our marriage, and keep us from tearing it down.

Whether in word or in deed may we seek to honor each other and glorify You.

Give us the strength to walk in sacrificial love, and a deep desire to press on in faith. Even on the days when it doesn't feel good to do so, may we continue to walk in Your will.

In the name of Jesus we pray. Amen.

Every wise woman buildeth her house: but the foolish plucketh it down with her hands.

Proverbs 14:1

TWENTY FOUR

To Endure

Dear Heavenly Father,

Give us the courage to follow Your will, and the strength to endure temptation.

Marriage is wonderful in so many ways, but some days it's harder than we ever imagined it could be.

We give into pride, we yield to temptation, we hold on to our anger, and we're selfish at times.

And so we're asking for the wisdom and strength to choose love. We're asking for the courage it takes to put down our pride and pick up the instruments of kindness and peace.

As brave and mighty warriors wait on the command of their captain, we yield our lives to Your will.

In the name of Jesus we pray. Amen.

I will love thee, O Lord, my strength. The Lord is my rock, and my fortress, and my deliverer; my God, my strength, in whom I will trust; my buckler, and the horn of my salvation, and my high tower. I will call upon the Lord, who is worthy to be praised: so shall I be saved from mine enemies.

Psalm 18:1-3

- TWENTY FIVE -

Home Dedication

Dear Heavenly Father,

We offer our home in dedication to You. May all that we have be fully consecrated to Your will.

Let our lives be a shining light, declaring Your glory and grace to all who visit our home.

Send Your angels to stand guard of each door and each window, keeping us safe from sickness and harm. And by the blood of Jesus may our home be fully cleansed.

Build a hedge of protection around these walls, rejecting all that is evil, and welcoming that which is good.

In the name of Jesus we pray. Amen.

There shall no evil befall thee, neither shall any plague come nigh thy dwelling. For he shall give his angels charge over thee, to keep thee in all thy ways. They shall bear thee up in their hands, lest thou dash thy foot against a stone.

Psalm 91:10-12

TWENTY SIX

In Tough Times

Dear Heavenly Father,

Thank You for entrusting us with the gift of marriage. I pray that we will never take it for granted or toss it aside without care.

Please teach us patience and give us the perseverance we need to get through the tough times. Remind us to press on when we feel like giving up, and to look forward when we feel like looking back.

Help us to stand guard of our marriage protecting it from any temptations that would draw us away from Your perfect will.

In the name of Jesus we pray. Amen.

Brethren, I count not myself to have apprehended: but this one thing I do, forgetting those things which are behind, and reaching forth unto those things which are before, I press toward the mark for the prize of the high calling of God in Christ Jesus.

Philippians 3:13-14

TWENTY SEVEN

Marriage Dedication

Dear Heavenly Father,

We come to You today with open hearts that long for more of You and less of us.

Placing our marriage before You, we dedicate every part of it to be used according to Your will, perfect timing, and wisdom.

Please show us the areas where we need to grow, and teach us how to pray for each other.

Give us the strength to release our grasp on this world as we grab hold of You.

May we pray without ceasing, moving forward in hope.

In the name of Jesus we pray. Amen.

Through wisdom is an house builded; and by understanding it is established: and by knowledge shall the chambers be filled with all precious and pleasant riches.

Proverbs 24:3-4

TWENTY EIGHT

To Communicate

Dear Heavenly Father,

Please teach us to communicate well. Give us hearts of understanding, compassion and love. Help us to listen more than we talk.

Your Word tells us that harsh words stir up anger and that a soft answer turns away wrath. Help us to remember this when we're frustrated, angry, and hurt.

Give us the patience we need to think before we speak, and give us the wisdom to choose words that edify one another.

May our words minister grace to each other, and above all may they glorify You.

In the name of Jesus we pray. Amen.

A soft answer turneth away wrath: but grievous words stir up anger. The tongue of the wise useth knowledge aright: but the mouth of fools poureth out foolishness.

Proverbs 15:1-2

- TWENTY NINE -
For Joy

Dear Heavenly Father,

May our lives be filled to overflowing with joy. Whether we're waiting on You for our next step or living according to plan, may we discover peace and joy that come to those who trust in Your will.

Give us the strength and courage to hold onto joy when others are dragging us down. For nobody can rob us of that which flows from Your Spirit.

It's not easy to rejoice in tribulation, or to give thanks when we experience loss, but all things are possible to those who believe. All things are beautiful to those who put their trust in Your hands.

In the name of Jesus we pray. Amen.

Wherein ye greatly rejoice, though now for a season, if need be, ye are in heaviness through manifold temptations: that the trial of your faith, being much more precious than of gold that perisheth, though it be tried with fire, might be found unto praise and honour and glory at the appearing of Jesus Christ: whom having not seen, ye love; in whom, though now ye see him not, yet believing, ye rejoice with joy unspeakable and full of glory.

1 Peter 1:6-8

THIRTY

For Unity

Dear Heavenly Father,

You have created us to be of one heart and one mind-- no longer two, we are joined together as one. Help us to strengthen this bond of unity.

May we hold fast to a faith that brings harmony to our marriage and life to our souls. For there is one bond and there is one hope for those who are unified by Your Spirit.

Let all selfishness be put away from us as we endeavor to live as husband and wife. And may we seek to walk in humility, as we put each other ahead of our selves.

In the name of Jesus we pray. Amen.

There is one body, and one Spirit, even as ye are called in one hope of your calling; One Lord, one faith, one baptism, one God and Father of all, who is above all, and through all, and in you all.

Ephesians 4:4-6

THIRTY ONE

To Lean on God's Strength

Dear Heavenly Father,

I pray that You would wrap Your arms around us and give us a sense of peace.

Remind us daily that You are in control, that You are powerful, and that You can do so much more than we could ever do on our own.

May we never forget how much we are loved, how precious we are in Your sight and how much You care for us.

Teach us to lean on You and to keep leaning on You. Restore our marriage according to Your will, and by Your power.

In the name of Jesus we pray. Amen.

Humble yourselves therefore under the mighty hand of God, that he may exalt you in due time: Casting all your care upon him; for he careth for you.

1 Peter 5:6-7

THIRTY TWO

To Shine

Dear Heavenly Father,

Please guide our steps. Help us to be a light in the dark world around us. Not merely professing our faith, but also proving our faith by the way that we live and the way that we love.

We pray that our marriage would be a testimony of Your compassionate kindness and mercy. May our words be seasoned with grace, and truth that breathes life into those around us.

Give us the wisdom to redeem the time that we have, proving all that is good, and acceptable according to Your perfect will.

In the name of Jesus we pray. Amen.

Ye are the light of the world. A city that is set on an hill cannot be hid. Neither do men light a candle, and put it under a bushel, but on a candlestick; and it giveth light unto all that are in the house. Let your light so shine before men, that they may see your good works, and glorify your Father which is in heaven.

Matthew 5:14-16

THIRTY THREE

For Good Health

Dear Heavenly Father,

Please grant us good health. Keep us safe from sickness and pain.

Our bodies are not our own--they are Yours, and every breath is given to us by Your grace. We are temples of Your Holy Ghost--purchased with a price and redeemed by the blood of Your Son Jesus Christ. May we never forget to treat ourselves with honor and care.

We bring our bodies to the foot of Your throne, believing You have the power to heal and the power to protect us according to Your will.

In the name of Jesus we pray. Amen.

Is any sick among you? let him call for the elders of the church; and let them pray over him, anointing him with oil in the name of the Lord: and the prayer of faith shall save the sick, and the Lord shall raise him up; and if he have committed sins, they shall be forgiven him. Confess your faults one to another, and pray one for another, that ye may be healed. The effectual fervent prayer of a righteous man availeth much.

James 5:14-16

THIRTY FOUR

To Forgive

Dear Heavenly Father,

Teach us to forgive. Your Word tells us to forgive each other as You forgive us.

We're reminded of His last moments on earth when Jesus cried out on behalf of those who crucified Him, "Father, forgive them; for they know not what they do."

In His deepest moment of sorrow, He loved.

But we're petty. We hang on to our hurt. We keep track of who's right and who's wrong. Ignoring the truth, we pamper our pride.

Give us the strength to let go of our pride and grab hold of grace.

Whether we're right or we're wrong, may we always choose love.

In the name of Jesus we pray. Amen.

For if ye forgive men their trespasses, your heavenly Father will also forgive you:

But if ye forgive not men their trespasses, neither will your Father forgive your trespasses.

Matthew 6:14-15

- THIRTY FIVE -

Our Thoughts

Dear Heavenly Father,

Your Word tells us that love beareth all things, believeth all things, hopeth all things, and endureth all things. But here we are, two imperfect people who are learning to love.

We'll never do everything right. In fact we'll do a lot of things wrong, which is why we need patience and kindness if we hope to endure.

May life-giving words take the place of fault-finding thoughts as we're planting seeds of encouragement.

Help us to let go of the expectations that are weighing us down, and teach us to anchor our lives with assurance and hope.

In the name of Jesus we pray. Amen.

Charity suffereth long, and is kind; charity envieth not; charity vaunteth not itself, is not puffed up, doth not behave itself unseemly, seeketh not her own, is not easily provoked, thinketh no evil; rejoiceth not in iniquity, but rejoiceth in the truth; beareth all things, believeth all things, hopeth all things, endureth all things.

1 Corinthians 13:4-7

- THIRTY SIX -
For Courage

Dear Heavenly Father,

We come before You today asking that You would teach us to walk in humility. Help us to see the importance of forgiveness and grace.

May we learn to love as You love, and to give up our right to be right.

Give us the courage to fight for our marriage and the valor to stand up for each other. Help us to lay down our pride, and to pick up the instruments of peace, kindness and grace.

Thank You for being the loving compassionate God that You are.

In the name of Jesus we pray. Amen.

At the same time came the disciples unto Jesus, saying, Who is the greatest in the kingdom of heaven?

And Jesus called a little child unto him, and set him in the midst of them,

And said, Verily I say unto you, Except ye be converted, and become as little children, ye shall not enter into the kingdom of heaven.

Whosoever therefore shall humble himself as this little child, the same is greatest in the kingdom of heaven.

Matthew 18:1-4

THIRTY SEVEN

Through Storms

Dear Heavenly Father,

Thank You for being our place of refuge and strength. Thank You for being the One we can lean on when life brings us down, and thank You for lifting us up.

Help us to keep our eyes focused on You when storms are heavy upon us. Please help us to find a sense of peace when our circumstances are anything but peaceful.

It's never easy to trust in Your will when it brings us down to our knees, but fear is soon washed away when our hope is in You.

In the name of Jesus we pray. Amen.

He maketh the storm a calm, so that the waves thereof are still. Then are they glad because they be quiet; so he bringeth them unto their desired haven. Oh that men would praise the Lord for his goodness, and for his wonderful works to the children of men!

Psalm 107:29-31

THIRTY EIGHT

Our Roles

Dear Heavenly Father,

Please remind us to pray for each other often, and to be kind as we're growing in grace.

Equip us to be the strength that we need, one for the other. May we serve to encourage as we fulfill our God-given roles; one a wise leader, and the other a compassionate help meet. For your Word says, "It is not good that the man should be alone; I will make him an help meet for him."

Thank You for Your wonderful gift of a trustworthy companion and friend. Thank you also for the gift of marriage that we open each day.

In the name of Jesus we pray. Amen.

And the Lord God caused a deep sleep to fall upon Adam, and he slept: and he took one of his ribs, and closed up the flesh instead thereof; And the rib, which the Lord God had taken from man, made he a woman, and brought her unto the man. And Adam said, This is now bone of my bones, and flesh of my flesh: she shall be called Woman, because she was taken out of Man.

Genesis 2:21-23

- THIRTY NINE -
For Protection

Dear Heavenly Father,

Let us draw closer to You, as we draw close to each other.

Keep us safe in your hands as we continue to grow strong in faith, choosing Your will for our marriage over our own. Whether it's easy or tough, I pray we choose well and walk away from temptation.

Please put a hedge of protection around us. Keep our marriage safe and secure under Your wing, and send Your angels to stand guard over us.

Thank You Lord, for all that You do and all that You are.

In the name of Jesus we pray. Amen.

But we have this treasure in earthen vessels, that the excellency of the power may be of God, and not of us.

We are troubled on every side, yet not distressed; we are perplexed, but not in despair;

Persecuted, but not forsaken; cast down, but not destroyed.

2 Corinthians 4:7-9

FORTY

Our Friendship

Dear Heavenly Father,

Please help us to nurture our friendship. Teach us what good friendship should look like and how we can build up this relationship daily.

Looking at the scriptures we see Jonathan and David, and how sacrifice was a vital part of their friendship. This doesn't come easy, Lord, which is why we need Your strength in our lives.

We see Ruth who was willing to step out in faith to follow Naomi. Leaving fear and uncertainty behind, she fiercely held on to the one that she loved.

Teach us to walk with a boldness of faith. And to always hold on to each other.

In the name of Jesus we pray. Amen.

And Ruth said, Intreat me not to leave thee, or to return from following after thee: for whither thou goest, I will go; and where thou lodgest, I will lodge: thy people shall be my people, and thy God my God: Where thou diest, will I die, and there will I be buried: the Lord do so to me, and more also, if ought but death part thee and me.

Ruth 1:16-17

- FORTY ONE -
Using Our Words

Dear Heavenly Father,

Our words hold great power. Some days they build up and encourage, while other days they tear down and destroy.

Please teach us to use them wisely.

The tongue is a mighty force. Help us to fine tune this instrument for Your glory and honor.

Grant us the wisdom to know when to speak and the right words to say.

May our words be seasoned with wisdom and grace. Let our voices ring forth with loving kindness and praise that builds up our marriage and unites us together as one.

In the name of Jesus we pray. Amen.

Let no corrupt communication proceed out of your mouth, but that which is good to the use of edifying, that it may minister grace unto the hearers.

Ephesians 4:29

FORTY TWO

To Serve Each Other

Dear Heavenly Father,

Help us to see each day as an opportunity to walk in humility and love; two servants with a desire to give more than we're given; two lovers willing to forgive before we're forgiven.

More of You, Lord. Less of us.

Let us be reminded of our Lord, Who lowered himself in the form of a servant to wash the feet of His disciples. May we also be willing servants who step down, lift up, let go, and hold on, according to Your perfect will.

In the name of Jesus we pray. Amen.

Ye call me Master and Lord: and ye say well; for so I am. If I then, your Lord and Master, have washed your feet; ye also ought to wash one another's feet. For I have given you an example, that ye should do as I have done to you.

John 13:13-15

FORTY THREE

To Strengthen Each Other

Dear Heavenly Father,

You've given us an amazing opportunity in this life. Not only to love each other, but to also share the good news of Your saving grace.

Please bless our marriage as we grow toward Christ-centered unity.

May we hunger and thirst for Your Word. And may that Word be a lamp to our feet and a light to our path.

If one should stumble, let the other be there for strength. And if one of us is weak may the other offer prayer and support.

As iron sharpens iron, help us to influence each other toward righteousness and truth.

In the name of Jesus we pray. Amen.

Two are better than one; because they have a good reward for their labour. For if they fall, the one will lift up his fellow: but woe to him that is alone when he falleth; for he hath not another to help him up. Again, if two lie together, then they have heat: but how can one be warm alone? And if one prevail against him, two shall withstand him; and a threefold cord is not quickly broken.

Ecclesiastes 4:9-12

- FORTY FOUR -
Anger and Pride

Dear Heavenly Father,

Thank you for the many times You patiently offer us grace.

Help us to choose truth when comfort is the easy way out, and to lean on Your strength when we're weak.

Remind us to be patient and kind when we're angry. Help us to walk in humility when all we want to do is hold on to our pride.

Teach us how to be a couple that loves at all times. Not just when it's easy or when it serves us, but when it's difficult to swallow our pride.

In the name of Jesus we pray. Amen.

A friend loveth at all times, and a brother is born for adversity.

Proverbs 17:17

- FORTY FIVE -
To Love

Dear Heavenly Father,

Please teach us to love the way You love, with patience, and kindness, and grace. Help us to love well on the good days and bad. Show us what agape love looks like between a husband and wife, and grant us the strength to lay down our pride for the good of our marriage.

Help us to walk the tough road together. Remind us to offer grace to each other when we're not being loved the way that we hoped that we would, and to bring that burden to prayer.

In the name of Jesus we pray. Amen.

And above all things have fervent charity among yourselves: for charity shall cover the multitude of sins.

1 Peter 4:8

- F O R T Y   S I X -
To Persevere

Dear Heavenly Father,

We live in a world where marriage is easily thrown to the side. Where people give up, and couples give in to temptation.

Please help us to recognize anything that might become a snare to us, and help us stand strong against the lure of temptation.

May we hold true to the vows that we made. Help us to love, honor and respect each other in the way that we should. Let us tenderly give of ourselves, in sickness and in health, forsaking all others, as long as we both shall live.

In the name of Jesus we pray. Amen.

Wherefore let him that thinketh he standeth take heed lest he fall. There hath no temptation taken you but such as is common to man: but God is faithful, who will not suffer you to be tempted above that ye are able; but will with the temptation also make a way to escape, that ye may be able to bear it.

1 Corinthians 10:12-13

FORTY SEVEN

For Virtue

Dear Heavenly Father,

Please help us to grow and mature in our faith.

Your word tells us to make every effort to add virtue to our faith and knowledge to our virtue, and so we're asking You, Lord to guide us as we're learning to grow.

Knowing that we want to mature is one thing, but exercising our faith takes patience and strength. Please grant us the strength to go the extra mile when it is required of us, and the wisdom to sit still when we should.

Thank you for your unfailing grace.

In the name of Jesus we pray. Amen.

And beside this, giving all diligence, add to your faith virtue; and to virtue knowledge; And to knowledge temperance; and to temperance patience; and to patience godliness; And to godliness brotherly kindness; and to brotherly kindness charity. For if these things be in you, and abound, they make you that ye shall neither be barren nor unfruitful in the knowledge of our Lord Jesus Christ.

2 Peter 1:5-8

FORTY EIGHT

For Compassion

Dear Heavenly Father,

Please teach us to walk in compassion and grace. Help to accept the fact that neither of us are perfect and that both of us are fighting a spiritual battle each and every day.

Yes, we will disappoint each other at times, which is why it's so important that we learn to love as you love.

We need wisdom in this area, Lord. We need humility, and we need strength. As You've poured out Your grace to us on the darkest of days, may we also pour grace out to others.

In the name of Jesus I pray. Amen.

As every man hath received the gift, even so minister the same one to another, as good stewards of the manifold grace of God.

1 Peter 4:10

- FORTY NINE -
For Wisdom

Dear Heavenly Father,

Please guide us through each path that we take, and give us the wisdom we need to make wise decisions together. May we grow with one heart and one mind, focused on doing Your will.

Please help us to take our eyes off of this world, and everything that pulls us toward it. For this earth is merely a place we're passing through on our way home.

May our marriage be a testimony to others of a bold inner faith. And may that faith wax stronger day after day.

In the name of Jesus we pray. Amen.

Knowing this, that the trying of your faith worketh patience. But let patience have her perfect work, that ye may be perfect and entire, wanting nothing. If any of you lack wisdom, let him ask of God, that giveth to all men liberally, and upbraideth not; and it shall be given him. James 1:3-5

FIFTY

To Overcome Temptation

Dear Heavenly Father,

There are so many ways that we want to grow, and things that we want to change, but we need self-control.

Grant us the strength to overcome temptation, for your word tells us that in all things we are more than conquerors.

Help us to control our tongues, our spending, our appetites, our anger, our lust, and our tempers. We need Your help, Lord, to bring our bodies under subjection to the Spirit.

May Your word sink into our hearts to guide us and keep us from sin, and may the power of Your Holy Spirit give us the strength to choose well.

In the name of Jesus we pray. Amen.

Do you not know that those who run in a race all run, but one receives the prize? Run in such a way that you may obtain it. And everyone who competes for the prize is temperate in all things. Now they do it to obtain a perishable crown, but we for an imperishable crown. Therefore I run thus: not with uncertainty. Thus I fight: not as one who beats the air. But I discipline my body and bring it into subjection, lest, when I have preached to others, I myself should become disqualified.

1 Corinthians 9:24-27

FIFTY ONE

To Listen Well

Dear Heavenly Father,

Please help us to listen well.

Teach us the importance of laying down our pride, so that we might communicate well.

Remind us to listen far more than we speak. And to not only listen, but seek to understand each other more than we do.

Help us to choose our words well so that we might encourage each other as we're growing together in grace.

Thank You for listening to us in the amazing way that You do. And, thank You for hearing our words time and again.

In the name of Jesus we pray. Amen.

Wherefore, my beloved brethren, let every man be swift to hear, slow to speak, slow to wrath: for the wrath of man worketh not the righteousness of God.

James 1:19-20

FIFTY TWO

Our Choices

Dear Heavenly Father,

Help us to make wise choices that bring glory and honor to You. When we're faced with a difficult situation, please give us the strength and the integrity to choose the right way over the easy way.

Give us a hunger for the word so we'll equip ourselves with wisdom. And may every choice we make be in line with Your Will.

Remind us to pray often, seeking Your guidance and truth. We want Your presence in our lives leading the way as we follow.

Surround us with friends who offer wise counsel. May they seek to serve You, more than their flesh and encourage us to serve also.

In the name of Jesus we pray. Amen.

Trust in the Lord with all thine heart; and lean not unto thine own understanding. In all thy ways acknowledge him, and he shall direct thy paths.

Proverbs 3:5-6

FIFTY THREE

Our Priorities

Dear Heavenly Father,

Please help us to set our priorities well. May we always put You first, and each other second.

It's easy to be drawn away by things that grab our attention and activities that tie up our time, and so we ask that You will give us the wisdom and strength to manage our time wisely.

May we take time out where it needs to be taken, so that we spend time with You and also each other.

Time is a gift we can either waste or use wisely. Please help us to manage it well, so we might bring glory to You and add strength to our marriage.

In the name of Jesus we pray. Amen.

Now it came to pass, as they went, that he entered into a certain village: and a certain woman named Martha received him into her house. And she had a sister called Mary, which also sat at Jesus' feet, and heard his word.

But Martha was cumbered about much serving, and came to him, and said, Lord, dost thou not care that my sister hath left me to serve alone? Bid her therefore that she help me.

And Jesus answered and said unto her, Martha, Martha, thou art careful and troubled about many things: but one thing is needful: and Mary hath chosen that good part, which shall not be taken away from her.

Luke 10:38-42

- F I F T Y   F O U R -
Our Attitudes

Dear Heavenly Father,

Please help us to shape our attitudes. We know that our attitudes can greatly affect each other, and we've seen how a good attitude can affect the rhythm of our home.

A good attitude can bring light and hope to a bad situation, it offers joy in the midst of sorrow. A good attitude can revive a weary soul, and a good attitude can inspire and motivate others. So we ask that you help us to choose well, Lord.

When we're faced with a choice, remind us to be happy, to be joyful, and to be thankful. In doing so, may our lives bring glory to You.

In the name of Jesus we pray. Amen.

A merry heart doeth good like a medicine: but a broken spirit drieth the bones.

Proverbs 17:22

- FIFTY FIVE -

For Stewardship

Dear Heavenly Father,

Thank You for each and every blessing that You have bestowed upon our marriage. May we never cease to thank You for Your gifts, or fail to see the beauty of Your grace.

Train us to be wise and generous stewards equipped with wisdom and self-control to manage our finances well. Help us to spend wisely, and teach us the importance of investing in our future.

May we learn to be just as content and thankful when finances are tight, as we are when we have plenty.

In the name of Jesus we pray. Amen.

Charge them that are rich in this world, that they be not highminded, nor trust in uncertain riches, but in the living God, who giveth us richly all things to enjoy; that they do good, that they be rich in good works, ready to distribute, willing to communicate.

1 Timothy 6:17-18

FIFTY SIX

Our Obedience

Dear Heavenly Father,

Our prayer today is that we will be obedient to Your will. Regardless of how tough decisions might be, our hope is that we will always choose Your wisdom over our own.

May we hunger and thirst after righteousness, and may we be doers of the word and not hearers only.

Give us the strength to bring our bodies into subjection to Your Spirit. Help us to bring both our thoughts and our actions into obedience to Your will.

And finally, grant us the strength to renew our minds daily, leaving the past behind, pressing forward in faith.

In the name of Jesus we pray. Amen.

For sin shall not have dominion over you: for ye are not under the law, but under grace.

What then? shall we sin, because we are not under the law, but under grace? God forbid.

Know ye not, that to whom ye yield yourselves servants to obey, his servants ye are to whom ye obey; whether of sin unto death, or of obedience unto righteousness?

Romans 6:14-16

FIFTY SEVEN

Through Trials

Dear Heavenly Father,

We pray that You would give us strength in the midst of trials.

Remind us to rejoice on the darkest of days knowing that the trying of our faith builds patience.

Teach us to lean on You and to put our trust in You at all times. For You have never failed us in the past and will never fail us in the future.

May we give thanks through every trial we have and in every situation we face, knowing that all things work together for good to them who are in Christ Jesus.

In the name of Jesus we pray. Amen.

And we know that all things work together for good to them that love God, to them who are the called according to his purpose.

Romans 8:28

FIFTY EIGHT

For Self-Control

Dear Heavenly Father,

Help us to exercise self-control in our lives. Without self-control our heart would be ruling our heads, and our feelings suppressing our faith.

And so Father we ask that you would give us the strength to do the right thing.

Help us to be self-controlled in every area of our lives.

For our bodies – that we would take care of them well.

For our minds – that we would be feeding them well.

For our tongues – that we would be using them well.

For our finances – that we would be investing them well.

And for our tempers – that we would be controlling them well.

May all that we do be handled with wisdom according to Your will for our lives.

In the name of Jesus we pray. Amen.

This I say then, Walk in the Spirit, and ye shall not fulfil the lust of the flesh.

For the flesh lusteth against the Spirit, and the Spirit against the flesh: and these are contrary the one to the other: so that ye cannot do the things that ye would.

But if ye be led of the Spirit, ye are not under the law.

Galatians 5:16-18

- FIFTY NINE -
Our Prayer Life

Dear Heavenly Father,

Thank You for this incredible opportunity that we have to kneel in Your presence. Thank you for the honor and the privilege of prayer. May there never be a day that we cease to bow our heads and give thanks for Your grace.

We ask that You lead us toward a toward a stronger prayer life. One in which we bring our marriage before You day after day. One in which we pray together, united by Your will.

May Your power always be the driving force in our lives.

In the name of Jesus we pray. Amen.

For we have not an high priest which cannot be touched with the feeling of our infirmities; but was in all points tempted like as we are, yet without sin.

Let us therefore come boldly unto the throne of grace, that we may obtain mercy, and find grace to help in time of need.

Hebrews 4:15-16

SIXTY

To Be Understanding

Dear Heavenly Father,

We pray for a deeper understanding of each other. We've been together for a while, but we're two different people who do things in two different ways. And so we ask that You'd give us the strength to be flexible when we need to be, and give us the patience to handle our emotions wisely.

Help us to be good listeners who are sensitive to the needs of each other.

May our differences sharpen each other to grow stronger in faith, and challenge each other to consider new things.

Bind us together in unity, and use our differences to strengthen that bond.

In the name of Jesus we pray. Amen.

For I say, through the grace given unto me, to every man that is among you, not to think of himself more highly than he ought to think; but to think soberly, according as God hath dealt to every man the measure of faith. For as we have many members in one body, and all members have not the same office: so we, being many, are one body in Christ, and every one members one of another.

Romans 12:3-5

- SIXTY ONE -
When We're Hurt

Dear Heavenly Father,

Please teach us to love those who hurt us. It's easy to love the ones who are kind and the ones who are gentle, but the challenge comes when we're called to love in difficult times.

Some days it feels as though we don't have the strength to love in a way that is pleasing to You, but You have taught us differently. You loved us before we loved You.

Guide our steps. Give us the strength to love as You do—with kindness, forgiveness, compassion, and grace.

Teach us to pray for them, Lord. Remind us to get down on our knees, leave our pain at the foot of Your throne, and rest in the knowledge that You're working on our behalf.

In the name of Jesus we pray. Amen.

Thus saith the LORD unto you, Be not afraid nor dismayed by reason of this great multitude; for the battle is not yours, but God's. To morrow go ye down against them: behold, they come up by the cliff of Ziz; and ye shall find them at the end of the brook, before the wilderness of Jeruel. Ye shall not need to fight in this battle: set yourselves, stand ye still, and see the salvation of the LORD with you, O Judah and Jerusalem: fear not, nor be dismayed; to morrow go out against them: for the LORD will be with you.

2 Chronicles 20:15–17

SIXTY TWO

Letting Go of Expectations

Dear Heavenly Father,

Thank you for this wonderful gift of marriage, and the opportunity that You have given us to be both lovers and friends.

We ask that You would guide and equip us to fulfill our roles as husband and wife. As we're growing in grace, teach us the best ways to support and encourage each other.

There will be days when we don't measure up to the expectations we hold, and so we ask that You help us to let go of those expectation and wisely choose love.

Let our eyes be constantly turned toward You, as we focus more on changing ourselves, and less on changing each other.

In the name of Jesus we pray. Amen.

And he spake a parable unto them, Can the blind lead the blind? shall they not both fall into the ditch?

The disciple is not above his master: but every one that is perfect shall be as his master. And why beholdest thou the mote that is in thy brother's eye, but perceivest not the beam that is in thine own eye?

Either how canst thou say to thy brother, Brother, let me pull out the mote that is in thine eye, when thou thyself beholdest not the beam that is in thine own eye? Thou hypocrite, cast out first the beam out of thine own eye, and then shalt thou see clearly to pull out the mote that is in thy brother's eye.

Luke 6:39-42

SIXTY THREE

Protect Our Marriage

Dear Heavenly Father,

Thank you for keeping us safe in Your hands, and close to Your heart.

We're thankful for your Word which reminds us how important it is to stand guard of our home, to watch over our marriage, and to protect our hearts from the enemy. We can't do this alone, Lord. We need Your help. We need Your power and grace. We need Your strength. We need You to lead us in wisdom to safety.

Help us to be watchmen who fiercely protect our marriage, and help us to guard it from harm.

In the name of Jesus we pray. Amen.

Be sober, be vigilant; because your adversary the devil, as a roaring lion, walketh about, seeking whom he may devour: Whom resist stedfast in the faith, knowing that the same afflictions are accomplished in your brethren that are in the world. But the God of all grace, who hath called us unto his eternal glory by Christ Jesus, after that ye have suffered a while, make you perfect, stablish, strengthen, settle you.

1 Peter 5:8-10

SIXTY FOUR

To Set Aside Distractions

Dear Heavenly Father,

Thank You for our marriage and for the home we have together.

Lord, You know that we're busy and how so many things compete for our time and attention.

We're asking You to help us set aside those distractions, so we can focus on connecting with each other and with You.

Please help us to make our house into a home. Help us to create an atmosphere that provides us with a sense of peace and togetherness.

Give us hearts that love each other more than we love the things that distract us. And give us the strength to choose well.

In the name of Jesus we pray. Amen.

But they that wait upon the Lord shall renew their strength; they shall mount up with wings as eagles; they shall run, and not be weary; and they shall walk, and not faint.

Isaiah 40:31

SIXTY FIVE

A Focus On God

Dear Heavenly Father,

We pray that You will help us to center our lives around You.

We're reminded in Your word that a strand of three cords is not quickly broken. We desire that strength in our marriage, and we know that nothing in this world can tear us apart when our lives are entwined in Your will.

Give us that focus, Lord. Turn our eyes away from the world and set them on You.

Teach us to not only hear the voice of our Shepherd but to follow Your voice in all that we do.

In the name of Jesus we pray. Amen.

Wherefore seeing we also are compassed about with so great a cloud of witnesses, let us lay aside every weight, and the sin which doth so easily beset us, and let us run with patience the race that is set before us,

Looking unto Jesus the author and finisher of our faith; who for the joy that was set before him endured the cross, despising the shame, and is set down at the right hand of the throne of God.

Hebrews 12:1-2

- S I X T Y S I X -
Standing Strong

Dear Heavenly Father,

We live in a world where many don't hold the same values we have for our marriage. So many don't believe the same way that we do when it comes to our faith.

Our lives are peculiar to those looking in, and our choices don't always make that much sense.

We're taking the unpopular route by following You, because we know it's the best route by far.

Please give us the courage to stand up for our faith when we're standing alone. Give us the strength to fight for our marriage when we're the only ones fighting. And give us the power to hold fast to our faith, when others let go.

In the name of Jesus we pray. Amen.

Unto you therefore which believe he is precious: but unto them which be disobedient, the stone which the builders disallowed, the same is made the head of the corner, and a stone of stumbling, and a rock of offence, even to them which stumble at the word, being disobedient: whereunto also they were appointed. But ye are a chosen generation, a royal priesthood, an holy nation, a peculiar people; that ye should shew forth the praises of him who hath called you out of darkness into his marvellous light.

1 Peter 2:7-9

SIXTY SEVEN

To Count Blessings

Dear Heavenly Father,

Give us the strength to count our blessings, even when things aren't going our way.

Remind us to stop. Right where we are. To take in the sweet scent of Your grace. There will be days that are darker than others. There will be times that are tough. But we trust in Your wisdom, Lord, and we trust that You are at work in our lives.

Open our eyes to the blessings at hand so that we might embrace each gift that we find there.

In the name of Jesus we pray. Amen.

And be not drunk with wine, wherein is excess; but be filled with the Spirit; speaking to yourselves in psalms and hymns and spiritual songs, singing and making melody in your heart to the Lord; giving thanks always for all things unto God and the Father in the name of our Lord Jesus Christ.

Ephesians 5:18-20

SIXTY EIGHT

To Be Tenderhearted

Dear Heavenly Father,

Teach us to be tenderhearted. Show us what that looks like in a marriage, and give us the strength to carry it through.

May we be compassionate lovers who are gentle and kind–lovers who choose their words wisely and handle their emotions with care.

It's easy to say things that sting when we're hurt and we're angry, but we're choosing a better path for our lives. Bitterness is a weed that should never take root in a marriage, lest it spring up again and again.

Give us a sweet spirit of kindness, and remove any resentment and hurt that has moved its way in.

In the name of Jesus we pray. Amen.

Let all bitterness, and wrath, and anger, and clamour, and evil speaking, be put away from you, with all malice: and be ye kind one to another, tenderhearted, forgiving one another, even as God for Christ's sake hath forgiven you.

Ephesians 4:31-32

- S I X T Y N I N E -
To Be Generous

Dear Heavenly Father,

Please help us to be a generous couple.

It's easier to hold onto the things we desire than it is to loosen our grip. It's easier to be self-centered than it is to be Christ-centered.

And so we ask that you give us the strength to open our hands and the compassion to open our eyes. Help us to see the needs that surround us. Help us to give.

May we be generous with our time. Giving it up for each other, and also to others in need.

May we be generous with our money. Spending wisely so we might give generously.

May we be generous with our hearts. Giving and forgiving as You forgive us.

In the name of Jesus we pray. Amen.

Give, and it shall be given unto you; good measure, pressed down, and shaken together, and running over, shall men give into your bosom. For with the same measure that ye mete withal it shall be measured to you again.

Luke 6:38

SEVENTY

To Take Pleasure in Each Other

Dear Heavenly Father,

May we always take pleasure in being together.

Marriage is a gift, and it's one that we never want to take for granted. Nor do we want to take each other for granted.

Your word tells us that a cheerful heart is good medicine. Experience tells us that laughter is best when it's shared with a friend.

And so we ask that you help us to nurture this part of our relationship, Lord. Help us to be a couple that delights in each other.

Teach us how to encourage each other, so we might be strong when we need it the most.

In the name of Jesus we pray. Amen.

Let thy fountain be blessed: and rejoice with the wife of thy youth.

Proverbs 5:18

SEVENTY ONE

To Grow

Dear Heavenly Father,

Please help us to grow. Give us the wisdom to put aside our desires for those things that we know to be good.

Grant us the strength to exercise the areas of our lives where we lack. Give us a focus and the perseverance to run.

May we step out in faith rather than sitting around waiting for motivation to move us. We know what we should be doing, and we know what we should be changing, but we're lacking self-discipline. Give us the wisdom to grow and the strength to move forward.

In the name of Jesus we pray. Amen.

As newborn babes, desire the sincere milk of the word, that ye may grow thereby.

1 Peter 2:2

SEVENTY TWO

To Value Each Other

Dear Heavenly Father,

Help us to appreciate the qualities we find in each other. Help us to value the everyday things that we might otherwise over look.

Thank you for creating us in each our own unique way. Equip us to use the gifts you have given us, and lead us to ways we can sharpen them both within ourselves and in each other.

Your word tells us how we were created with intent, and how we're fearfully and wonderfully made. Help us to appreciate these gifts that you have knit into our souls.

In the name of Jesus we pray. Amen.

I will praise thee; for I am fearfully and wonderfully made: marvellous are thy works; and that my soul knoweth right well. My substance was not hid from thee, when I was made in secret, and curiously wrought in the lowest parts of the earth. Thine eyes did see my substance, yet being unperfect; and in thy book all my members were written, which in continuance were fashioned, when as yet there was none of them.

Psalm 139:14-16

- SEVENTY THREE -
Leave Burdens Behind Us

Dear Heavenly Father,

Please help us to heal. Take each broken part, and breathe life into it.

Help us to get past the sting of our pain and to find new ways to rebuild our future.

We can't forget those things that have hurt us, but we can forgive and we can move forward in faith.

Help us to leave our burdens behind us; to trust in Your authority, and to rely on Your justice.

Give us the strength to release our pain into Your almighty hands, knowing that You are able to do abundantly more than we ever could on our own.

In the name of Jesus we pray. Amen.

If it be possible, as much as lieth in you, live peaceably with all men.

Dearly beloved, avenge not yourselves, but rather give place unto wrath: for it is written, Vengeance is mine; I will repay, saith the Lord.

Therefore if thine enemy hunger, feed him; if he thirst, give him drink: for in so doing thou shalt heap coals of fire on his head.

Be not overcome of evil, but overcome evil with good. – Romans 12:18-21

- S E V E N T Y   F O U R -
To Speak Kindly

Dear Heavenly Father,

Teach us to speak kindly to each other, or to not speak at all. Give us the strength to lay down our pride, and the virtue to exercise patience.

May we listen far more than we speak, and seek to understand each other more than we do.

Help us to choose our words wisely so that we might build up and encourage each other, instead of tearing each other down.

We can't take back unkind words that were spoken, but we can choose to speak kindly today.

In the name of Jesus we pray. Amen.

A good man out of the good treasure of the heart bringeth forth good things: and an evil man out of the evil treasure bringeth forth evil things.

But I say unto you, That every idle word that men shall speak, they shall give account thereof in the day of judgment.

Matthew 12:35-36

SEVENTY FIVE

That Nothing Would Divide Us

Dear Heavenly Father,

We come before you today asking that You would protect our marriage. Your word tells us that we are no longer two, but that we are one flesh. And so we ask that nothing would divide us.

Grant us the courage to stand strong when we're facing a storm. Whether we're up against poverty, sickness, unemployment, temptation, or stress, give us the strength to face it together.

We want to grow old together. We want to be holding hands long after old age has set in. We want to be a couple that prays together and stays together until You call us home.

In the name of Jesus we pray. Amen.

And he answered and said unto them, Have ye not read, that he which made them at the beginning made them male and female,

And said, For this cause shall a man leave father and mother, and shall cleave to his wife: and they twain shall be one flesh?

Wherefore they are no more twain, but one flesh. What therefore God hath joined together, let not man put asunder.

Matthew 19:4-6

SEVENTY SIX

Ignite Passion Between Us

Dear Heavenly Father,

Please help us to reconnect. Remind us of the many things we fell in love with, and ignite the passion between us.

We haven't fallen out of love, but sometimes we're pulled in two different directions. Some days we're so busy keeping up with it all, that we barely make time for each other. Some days we forget the reasons we fell in love in the first place.

Help us to see, and give us the strength to remove, anything that is standing between us. Give us the perseverance to pursue each other with a fervent love.

Rekindle this flame, Lord, and help us to keep it alive.

In the name of Jesus we pray. Amen.

Seeing ye have purified your souls in obeying the truth through the Spirit unto unfeigned love of the brethren, see that ye love one another with a pure heart fervently.

1 Peter 1:22

- SEVENTY SEVEN -
Draw Closer to God

Dear Heavenly Father,

Our prayer today is that we would grow closer to you.

Give us a burning desire to spend time in Your presence. And give us the patience to stay there.

Help us to see the importance of prayer, and to make it a priority in our lives.

Give us a hunger for Your Word. Not so that we might gain knowledge from reading it, but that we would gain an understanding of You and Your will.

We invite You into Our marriage, not as our guest, but as our friend, our companion, our Lord.

In the name of Jesus we pray. Amen.

Let us draw near with a true heart in full assurance of faith, having our hearts sprinkled from an evil conscience, and our bodies washed with pure water.

Let us hold fast the profession of our faith without wavering; (for he is faithful that promised;)

And let us consider one another to provoke unto love and to good works.

Hebrews 10:22-24

SEVENTY EIGHT

Surrender Our Weaknesses

Dear Heavenly Father,

We come before Your throne of grace and lay our marriage at Your feet. You see our struggles, You know our hearts, You see the many times we fail. Yet by Your grace and with Your strength we grow.

All praise to You.

We ask that You strengthen us and enable us to fulfill our vows and to be the husband and wife You desire us to be.

We know that You equip the ones You call, Lord, and so we surrender our weaknesses to You in faith. Please strengthen us and use us according to Your will.

In the name of Jesus we pray. Amen.

Hast thou not known? hast thou not heard, that the everlasting God, the Lord, the Creator of the ends of the earth, fainteth not, neither is weary? there is no searching of his understanding.

He giveth power to the faint; and to them that have no might he increaseth strength.

Even the youths shall faint and be weary, and the young men shall utterly fall: but they that wait upon the Lord shall renew their strength; they shall mount up with wings as eagles; they shall run, and not be weary; and they shall walk, and not faint.

Isaiah 40:28-31

SEVENTY NINE

A Victorious Life in Christ

Dear Heavenly Father,

Give us the confidence to stand up for what we believe in and the strength to carry on Your work even when it's hard to do so.

When we're weak, be our strength. When we're lost, be our light. When we're afraid, grant us courage. When we're unsure, give us faith.

Guide us and direct our lives according to Your will. Our desire is to have a Christ-centered marriage, to love as You love, and to stand pure before You.

Give us clean hands and a pure heart, that we might live victoriously through faith in Jesus Christ.

In His name we pray. Amen.

Thanks be to God, which giveth us the victory through our Lord Jesus Christ. Therefore, my beloved brethren, be ye stedfast, unmoveable, always abounding in the work of the Lord, forasmuch as ye know that your labour is not in vain in the Lord.

1 Corinthians 15:57-58

EIGHTY

To Live a Sacrificial Life

Dear Heavenly Father,

We want our lives to be centered on You, everything we do to bring glory to You, and everything we say to bring honor to You. But unless we're living a sacrificial life, pride will always get in the way.

It's easier to be selfish than it is to be selfless.

It's easier to hold onto our anger than it is to walk in humility.

It's easier to lose our temper than it is to be patient.

It's easier to speak our mind than it is to hold your tongue.

But we're not choosing an easy life, Lord. We're choosing to love.

Please give us the strength to fulfill our vows, to carry our cross, and to walk in Your will.

In the name of Jesus we pray. Amen.

I beseech you therefore, brethren, by the mercies of God, that ye present your bodies a living sacrifice, holy, acceptable unto God, which is your reasonable service.

And be not conformed to this world: but be ye transformed by the renewing of your mind, that ye may prove what is that good, and acceptable, and perfect, will of God.

Romans 12:1-2

EIGHTY ONE

Love Without Keeping Score

Dear Heavenly Father,

Please teach us to love and to serve the people that you have put in our lives. Help us to grow in the likeness of Jesus Who came to serve rather than to be served.

May we live beyond ourselves, serving and loving each other without keeping score—giving to others without the hope of acclamation or expectation of return.

Help us to see the beauty in serving. Allow us to be Your hands and Your feet in this world.

In the name of Jesus we pray. Amen.

Look not every man on his own things, but every man also on the things of others. Let this mind be in you, which was also in Christ Jesus: who, being in the form of God, thought it not robbery to be equal with God: but made himself of no reputation, and took upon him the form of a servant, and was made in the likeness of men: and being found in fashion as a man, he humbled himself, and became obedient unto death, even the death of the cross.

Philippians 2:4-8

EIGHTY TWO

Trust in His Timing

Dear Heavenly Father,

Please teach us to wait on Your timing and to be content with what comes our way.

Your word tells us that there is a season and a time for every purpose under heaven.

As difficult as some of those seasons might be, we trust that You will carry us through. The waiting is hard, but we're learning to trust in Your timing and Your perfect will.

Whether we're sick or we're healthy, we're rich or we're poor, we're facing a trial, or everything is going our way—teach us to rejoice in Your goodness.

Teach us to wait, to hold on to hope, and to fiercely hold on to our faith.

In the name of Jesus we pray. Amen.

To every thing there is a season, and a time to every purpose under the heaven:

a time to be born, and a time to die; a time to plant, and a time to pluck up that which is planted; a time to kill, and a time to heal; a time to break down, and a time to build up; a time to weep, and a time to laugh; a time to mourn, and a time to dance; a time to cast away stones, and a time to gather stones together; a time to embrace, and a time to refrain from embracing; atime to get, and a time to lose; a time to keep, and a time to cast away; atime to rend, and a time to sew; a time to keep silence, and a time to speak; a time to love, and a time to hate; a time of war, and a time of peace.

Ecclesiastes 3:1-8

- EIGHTY THREE -
A Safe Place For Each Other

Dear Heavenly Father,

A good friend is someone you can run to in times of trouble. A good friend is someone you can trust with your heart. A good friend is someone who finds you in the dark and carries you back to the light.

Help us to be that friend. Help us to be a safe place for each other.

Teach us to handle each other with care. Give us the wisdom to encourage each other, and give us the right words to say that we might uplift and edify one another.

And finally, thank You for being our safe place of protection and strength.

In the name of Jesus we pray. Amen.

He shall cover thee with his feathers, and under his wings shalt thou trust: his truth shall be thy shield and buckler. Thou shalt not be afraid for the terror by night; nor for the arrow that flieth by day; nor for the pestilence that walketh in darkness; nor for the destruction that wasteth at noonday.

A thousand shall fall at thy side, and ten thousand at thy right hand; but it shall not come nigh thee.

Psalm 91:4-7

- EIGHTY FOUR -
Turning Our Back on This World

Dear Heavenly Father,

Help us to grow with faith-focused determination. Give us the strength according to Your glorious power to turn our back on this world when we're called to.

Grant us patience and courage to walk in Your will, and to live out our mission.

May ours be a Christ-centered marriage that brings glory to You in the way that we love. Equip us to be servants of grace who give more than we're given and forgive before we're forgiven.

In the name of Jesus we pray. Amen.

And Jesus, walking by the sea of Galilee, saw two brethren, Simon called Peter, and Andrew his brother, casting a net into the sea: for they were fishers.

And he saith unto them, Follow me, and I will make you fishers of men.

And they straightway left their nets, and followed him.

Matthew 4:18-20

EIGHTY FIVE

Facing Disappointments

Dear Heavenly Father,

It's easier to soar on a mountain than it is to hike through the valley. It's easier to worry than it is to trust. Life is full of ups and downs, and so we ask for Your strength to carry us through.

Teach us to dance in the rain. Help us to face disappointments with unwavering faith.

Your word tells us that weeping may endure for a night, but joy comes in the morning.

We know that all things work together for good to those who love You and are called according to Your purpose.

Give us the courage to wait on that promise, and the patience to trust in Your will.

In the name of Jesus we pray. Amen.

For my thoughts are not your thoughts, neither are your ways my ways, saith the Lord.

For as the heavens are higher than the earth, so are my ways higher than your ways, and my thoughts than your thoughts.

Isaiah 55:8-9

EIGHTY SIX

Inviting the Holy Spirit In

Dear Heavenly Father,

We come before You—two servants ready to be used according to Your will.

You know the most intimate parts of our lives. You've seen the struggles we've had. You know we have habits that we need to change, and things we need to let go of.

When we are weak You are strong. Where we fail, You succeed. When we stumble You reach down to pull us back up.

Be our fortress, our strength, and our stronghold. We can't do this alone, Lord. We need Your mighty hand at work in our lives. And so we invite Your Holy Spirit to move in our hearts, that we might walk in Your power and strength.

In the name of Jesus we pray. Amen.

Now the God of peace, that brought again from the dead our Lord Jesus, that great shepherd of the sheep, through the blood of the everlasting covenant, make you perfect in every good work to do his will, working in you that which is well pleasing in his sight, through Jesus Christ; to whom be glory for ever and ever. Amen.

Hebrews 13:20-21

- EIGHTY SEVEN -
Purify Our Hearts

Dear Heavenly Father,

There's beauty in the words of David who wrote, "Let the words of my mouth, and the meditation of my heart, be acceptable in thy sight" (Psalm 19:14). David understood that the heart has a great influence on the tongue.

That's our prayer too, Lord. Purify our hearts. Teach us to protect them. Help us to sift through those things that we allow into our minds, so that we might meditate on that which is good for the soul.

Grant us the wisdom to nurture our thoughts, to fill them with truth, and to fortify them with prayer.

In the name of Jesus we pray. Amen.

For a good tree bringeth not forth corrupt fruit; neither doth a corrupt tree bring forth good fruit.

For every tree is known by his own fruit. For of thorns men do not gather figs, nor of a bramble bush gather they grapes.

A good man out of the good treasure of his heart bringeth forth that which is good; and an evil man out of the evil treasure of his heart bringeth forth that which is evil: for of the abundance of the heart his mouth speaketh.

Luke 6:43-45

EIGHTY EIGHT

Living in Harmony With Difficult People

Dear Heavenly Father,

Please help us to be compassionate and understanding toward others. Give us the patience to live in harmony with difficult people.

It's easy to be self-centered, but we want to be Christ-centered. We want to reach out to people to love as You love.

Remind us to slow down for others, and to take time out to say hello or to lend a helping hand.

Grant us the strength to put on kindness when we least feel like it, and the wisdom to know when to step forward and when to pull back.

In the name of Jesus we pray. Amen.

But I say unto you, Love your enemies, bless them that curse you, do good to them that hate you, and pray for them which despitefully use you, and persecute you; that ye may be the children of your Father which is in heaven: for he maketh his sun to rise on the evil and on the good, and sendeth rain on the just and on the unjust.

For if ye love them which love you, what reward have ye? do not even the publicans the same? And if ye salute your brethren only, what do ye more than others? do not even the publicans so?

Be ye therefore perfect, even as your Father which is in heaven is perfect.

Matthew 5:44-48

EIGHTY NINE

To Build Teamwork

Dear Heavenly Father,

Help us to build teamwork in our marriage. Bind us together with one heart and one mind so that we might work together, fulfilling our purpose.

Sometimes it feels easier to work alone than it is to work together, but we see in Your word that two are better than one. Marriage is strengthened when we're pulling together.

Teach us to use our gifts in harmony with the other, like two hands working together as one.

May we both esteem the each other higher than ourselves, and may we be patient as we're growing together in grace.

In the name of Jesus we pray. Amen.

Fulfil ye my joy, that ye be likeminded, having the same love, being of one accord, of one mind.

Let nothing be done through strife or vainglory; but in lowliness of mind let each esteem other better than themselves.

Look not every man on his own things, but every man also on the things of others.

Philippians 2:2-4

NINETY

To Inspire Each Other

Dear Heavenly Father,

Help us to inspire the best in each other.

May our love and encouragement spur each other on to growth and good works, and may we provoke a sense of worth in each other.

When we inspire someone, we breathe life into them. When we discourage others, we drain them. Help us to be that life breathing force.

Help us to reinforce the work You have called us to do by supporting each other in prayer, and edifying one another with our words.

May we stand at the sidelines cheering each other on to be the best we can be, and may it all be done for Your glory.

In the name of Jesus we pray. Amen.

A continual dropping in a very rainy day and a contentious woman are alike. Whosoever hideth her hideth the wind, and the ointment of his right hand, which bewrayeth itself.

Iron sharpeneth iron; so a man sharpeneth the countenance of his friend.

Proverbs 27: 15-17

NINETY ONE

Treasure Our Marriage More Than Our Ego

Dear Heavenly Father,

May we treasure our marriage more than we treasure our ego.

Grant us the power to break the chains of self-importance and pride, and give us the courage to walk in Your Spirit when our flesh tries to stand in the way.

If we should stumble and fall, give us the strength it takes to walk in humility, to admit that we've made a mistake, and to get back to work on repairing our marriage.

Teach us to take the focus off of our selves, and to focus our marriage on You.

In the name of Jesus we pray. Amen.

Pride goeth before destruction, and an haughty spirit before a fall.

Better it is to be of an humble spirit with the lowly, than to divide the spoil with the proud.

Proverbs 16:18-19

NINETY TWO

When We're Weak

Dear Heavenly Father,

Give us faith. Teach us to trust You in our darkest moments and to lean on Your strength when we're weak.

And if we have days when we don't sense your presence, help us to exercise faith. Give us the strength to rejoice in tribulation, and the courage to trust that You will be the same faithful God tomorrow that You were in the past.

Our marriage vows aren't merely for us, Lord. They are also a symbol of our dedication to You. Take every part of this marriage, for better, for worse, for richer, for poorer, in sickness and in health to do as You will.

And may we be faithful to You all of our days on this earth.

In the name of Jesus we pray. Amen.

Let not mercy and truth forsake thee: bind them about thy neck; write them upon the table of thine heart: so shalt thou find favour and good understanding in the sight of God and man.

Trust in the Lord with all thine heart; and lean not unto thine own understanding.

In all thy ways acknowledge him, and he shall direct thy paths.

Proverbs 3:3-6

NINETY THREE

To Defend Each Other's Honor

Dear Heavenly Father,

We come before You today asking that You would help us to defend each other's honor.

Keep us from saying anything negative about each other, unless it's for the sake or hope of restoration.

If there is any disrespect on our part or on the part of another, may it not be tolerated, but gently corrected.

Give us the courage to stand up for each other, and the wisdom to be supportive.

When we're speaking to others, remind us to look for and to illustrate the goodness we find in our spouse.

As quickly and willing as we are to defend our self, may we each protect the one that we love.

In the name of Jesus we pray. Amen.

Who can find a virtuous woman? for her price is far above rubies. The heart of her husband doth safely trust in her, so that he shall have no need of spoil. She will do him good and not evil all the days of her life.

Proverbs 31:10-12

NINETY FOUR

Protection From the Enemy

Dear Heavenly Father,

One spark can set a field on fire, one spark can ignite greatness, and one spark can change the course of our marriage. Ignite that spark, Lord. Give us a passion to fight for our marriage.

We can either look for the worst in our spouse or we can choose to see the best in each other. We can let the little things bring us down, or we can choose to give thanks for the blessings we have. Help us to choose well.

Give us life in abundance. Protect our marriage from the enemy. Don't let anything in this world steal our joy, kill our passion, or destroy our marriage.

In the name of Jesus we pray. Amen.

The thief cometh not, but for to steal, and to kill, and to destroy: I am come that they might have life, and that they might have it more abundantly.

John 10:10

NINETY FIVE

To Joyfully Serve

Dear Heavenly Father,

Your word tells us to serve one another in love. It tells us that that whatever we do for others should be done as unto You.

And so our desire today is to joyfully serve one another as unto You.

Give us an awareness of the ways we can serve each other in love. Give us a good attitude, so that we don't merely love for the sake of our vows, but for Your sake, Lord.

Grant us the knowledge to see were we can help and how we can best help one another.

We have the opportunity to work as a team, and to lighten the load.

May we seize those opportunities with joy.

In the name of Jesus we pray. Amen.

And whatsoever ye do, do it heartily, as to the Lord, and not unto men; knowing that of the Lord ye shall receive the reward of the inheritance: for ye serve the Lord Christ.

Colossians 3:23-24

NINETY SIX

To Stop Pointing Fingers

Dear Heavenly Father,

It's natural to want to point fingers. It's easy to push your frustration off on somebody else.

What isn't so easy to do is to step back from a situation to examine our own hearts.

Grant us the humility to accept responsibility. Grant us the strength to take the next step toward change.

If we need to apologize, let us take care of that quickly. If we need to forgive, bring us down to our knees asking for humility and wisdom to guide us. And if we need to reconcile our differences, bring us both to that place of open honesty where we can join hands in prayer, and move forward together.

In the name of Jesus we pray. Amen.

Charity suffereth long, and is kind; charity envieth not; charity vaunteth not itself, is not puffed up, doth not behave itself unseemly, seeketh not her own, is not easily provoked, thinketh no evil; rejoiceth not in iniquity, but rejoiceth in the truth; beareth all things, believeth all things, hopeth all things, endureth all things.

1 Corinthians 13:4-7

NINETY SEVEN

A Wife's Prayer For Her Husband

Dear Heavenly Father,

I bring my husband before You today asking that You would bless him and shape him into the man he was designed to be.

Give him strength to lead our family, as Christ led the church with love and humility.

Equip him with wisdom to make good decisions that are pleasing to you.

Show him his worth, Lord. And show me ways that I might edify him.

Please protect his job, give him a peaceful work environment, and secure the position he has.

Grant him the patience and understanding he needs to love me the way that he should.

In the name of Jesus I pray. Amen.

Likewise, ye wives, be in subjection to your own husbands; that, if any obey not the word, they also may without the word be won by the conversation of the wives; while they behold your chaste conversation coupled with fear.

Whose adorning let it not be that outward adorning of plaiting the hair, and of wearing of gold, or of putting on of apparel;

1 Peter 3:1-3

NINETY EIGHT

A Husband's Prayer For His Wife

Dear Heavenly Father,

I bring my wife before you today asking that you would bless her and shape her into the woman she was designed to be.

Help her to see her worth and her beauty the way that I do.

Bring good friends into her life. Women she can laugh with, women who encourage her, and women who are there when she needs good advice.

Develop her talents and show me ways that I might encourage and nurture her interests.

Give her the wisdom and strength to balance her time, and show me the ways I might help her.

Grant her the patience and understanding she needs to love me the way that she should.

In the name of Jesus I pray. Amen.

Fulfil ye my joy that ye be likeminded, having the same love, being of one accord, of one mind. Let nothing be done through strife or vainglory; but in lowliness of mind let each esteem other better than themselves. Look not every man on his own things, but every man also on the things of others.Philippians 2:2-4

NINETY NINE

A Wife's Prayer For Her Husband (2)

Dear Heavenly Father,

Thank you for this wonderful gift of a husband, companion and friend. Remind me to celebrate his achievements, and to turn my focus away from his faults.

Equip me to be the help meet you have called me to be, and the friend my husband needs me to be.

Help me to recognize his efforts, his courage, his strength, and to sing his praises in a way that brings honor to him and to our marriage.

Lead me to love. Teach me to speak kindly when I'm frustrated, and to respect him as the head of our home.

Show me the ways that I might encourage and support Him to be the man you have called him to be.

In the name of Jesus I pray. Amen.

Wives, submit yourselves unto your own husbands, as unto the Lord. For the husband is the head of the wife, even as Christ is the head of the church: and he is the saviour of the body.

Therefore as the church is subject unto Christ, so let the wives be to their own husbands in every thing.

Ephesians 5:22-24

A Husband's Prayer For His Wife (2)

Dear Heavenly Father,

Thank you for this gracious gift of a wife, companion and friend. May I celebrate her achievements, and turn my focus away from her faults.

Teach me to love, honor, and cherish my wife as Christ loved and gave Himself up for us. Give me the courage to protect her, and the wisdom to lead.

Help me to recognize her efforts, her courage, her strengths, and to sing her praises in a way that bring honor to her and our marriage. Lead me to love.

Remind me to pray for her daily, that she might grow strong in Your grace.

In the name of Jesus I pray Amen.

Husbands, love your wives, even as Christ also loved the church, and gave himself for it; that he might sanctify and cleanse it with the washing of water by the word, that he might present it to himself a glorious church, not having spot, or wrinkle, or any such thing; but that it should be holy and without blemish.

So ought men to love their wives as their own bodies. He that loveth his wife loveth himself.

Ephesians 5:25-28

About the Author:

Darlene Schacht, is known by her readers as The Time-Warp Wife. She's is an Evangelical Christian whose number one priority is to serve Jesus Christ in every area of her life. She and her husband Michael live in Manitoba Canada. Married 26 years, they have four children (three still at home), a bird and a pug.

Their lives are basically surrounded with three things: faith, music and everything books.

She's an award winning and New York Times best-selling author through a book she co-authored with actress Candace Cameron Bure, Reshaping it All.

Her articles have been featured at KirkCameron.com, FortheFamily.Org, and WomenLivingWell.org

Find Darlene on the web here:
Blog: TimeWarpWife.com
Facebook: timewarpwife
Twitter: timewarpwife
Pinterest: timewarpwife

If you enjoyed this book, please leave a review at Amazon.

Made in the USA
Lexington, KY
22 August 2015